Original Title: 101 STRANGE BUT TRUE NFL FACTS

©101 STRANGE BUT TRUE NFL FACTS, Carlos
Martínez Cerdá and Victor Martínez Cerdá, 2023

Authors: Victor Martínez Cerdá and Carlos
Martínez Cerdá (V&C Brothers)

© Cover and illustrations: V&C Brothers

Layout and design: V&C Brothers

101
STRANGE BUT TRUE
NFL FACTS

INCREDIBLE AND
SURPRISING EVENTS

1

Before the creation of specific protections for American football, players improvised with different materials to protect their bodies during games.

One of the most common forms of homemade protection was using thick magazines or rolled-up newspapers around the shins to prevent injuries.

These improvised shin guards were tied with adhesive tape or laces and placed under the player's socks.

Although not very effective, they offered some protection against impacts and scrapes.

Other forms of homemade protection, such as shoulder pads made from rolled-up towels or improvised masks to protect the face, were also used.

These improvised materials were often uncomfortable and ineffective, which led to the creation of specific protections for American football.

The first specific protections for American football included leather helmets and padded shoulder pads, but over time, other types of protections were developed, such as hip, thigh, and shin protections.

These protections were much more effective than improvised ones and helped reduce the number of injuries in the sport.

2

During the early 20th century, American football was considered by many to be a dangerous and violent sport.

There were concerns about the number of injuries that occurred during games, including bone fractures and concussions, and many people called for the sport to be banned.

In this context, President Theodore Roosevelt met with leaders from the American football community to discuss the sport and seek solutions to reduce the risk of injuries.

As a former college football player, Roosevelt appreciated the value of the sport and wanted to find a way to make it safer for players.

In 1905, after a series of serious injuries and deaths on the field, Roosevelt convened a meeting of college football leaders to discuss the sport and find solutions to reduce the risk of injuries.

The meeting led to the creation of the National Collegiate Athletic Association (NCAA), which established rules and safety measures for the sport.

Among the safety measures implemented by the NCAA were the elimination of the most dangerous tactics of the game, such as high tackling and the prohibition of blocking from behind.

New protective equipment, such as padded helmets and shoulder pads, were also introduced to reduce the risk of injuries to the head and shoulders.

Roosevelt's leadership and support for the reform of American football helped change the perception of the sport and save it from being banned.

Today, American football remains a popular sport in the United States and has continued to evolve to make it safer for players.

3

American football has often been considered a sport that prepares young people for military careers due to its physical and mental demands.

Many schools and universities have used American football as part of their training program for future soldiers and officers.

The physical demands of American football are one of the reasons why it is considered a useful sport to prepare young people for a military career.

The game requires a combination of strength, speed, endurance, and agility, as well as mental skills such as the ability to think quickly and make quick decisions under pressure.

These skills are fundamental on the battlefield, where endurance and the ability to maintain concentration are key to survival.

Additionally, American football fosters values such as teamwork, discipline, leadership, and perseverance, which are also very important in the military field.

American football players learn to work together towards a common goal, follow orders, and overcome obstacles and difficulties.

For these reasons, many schools and universities have used American football as a tool to prepare young people for a military career.

In fact, some American football players have gone on to become military personnel after their sporting career, and many have commented that the experience of playing American football prepared them for the demands of their military career.

4

American football originated as a collegiate and club sport in the United States, in which players participated for fun and without receiving any financial compensation.

However, as the sport became more popular, teams began to pay talented players to join their ranks, marking the beginning of professional American football.

The first player known to have received a salary for playing American football was William "Pudge" Heffelfinger in 1892.

Heffelfinger was a star player at Yale University and was hired by the Allegheny Athletic Association team to play a game against the rival Pittsburgh team.

In exchange for playing in that game, Heffelfinger received $500.

This payment marked a milestone in the history of American football, as it was the first time a player received financial compensation for playing.

At that time, the practice of paying players was not allowed by the sport's rules, but this did not prevent teams from continuing to hire professional players to improve their chances of winning.

Over time, the practice of paying players became increasingly common in American football, and in 1920 the National Football League (NFL) was founded, which became the main organization of professional American football in the United States.

Since then, player salaries have increased significantly, and currently, the best players can earn millions of dollars per year.

5

During the early years of professional American football, which began in the late 19th and early 20th centuries, there was no limit to the number of changes a player could make between teams.

Players were not tied to any specific club or team through contracts and could change teams at any time, even in the middle of the season.

This lack of restrictions led to great player mobility, and there were often changes between teams in search of better opportunities or a higher salary.

In addition, teams often competed against each other for the best players, offering higher salaries and additional benefits to attract players to their ranks.

In 1920, the National Football League (NFL) was founded, which introduced a system of contracts for players, which limited player mobility between teams.

From that moment on, players could no longer change teams freely and without restrictions and were bound by a contract with a specific team.

The introduction of contracts also established a more stable salary structure and allowed teams to retain the most talented players for longer periods of time.

6

In the early 20th century, American football faced a safety crisis after several deaths and serious injuries occurred on the field.

In 1905, there were a total of 18 deaths related to American football due to head, neck, and spinal injuries.

This led to a national debate about the safety of the sport and a call for stricter safety measures.

7

The history behind the oval shape of the American football is somewhat uncertain, but it is believed to be partly due to an accident.

During the early years of the game, the ball used was more round, similar to that used in soccer.

However, over time, players began to experiment with different shapes and sizes of ball to better adapt them to the game.

The oval shape of the American football is believed to have originated in a game played in 1869 between Princeton and Rutgers universities.

According to legend, the ball that was brought for the game was deflated, so the players had to inflate it by hand.

Unable to fully inflate it evenly, the ball ended up with an oval and uneven shape.

Although this incident may have contributed to the current shape of the American football, it is likely that the evolution of the ball's shape was a gradual process and not something that happened overnight.

Additionally, the oval shape of the ball may also be due to the need for the ball to be thrown with greater accuracy and distance, and to be more easily gripped by players during the game.

8

**Canada played an important role in the development
of the rules of modern American football.**

In the 1860s, the game played in the United States resembled
rugby more than the American football we know today.

Players could grab and run with the ball and there were no downs limit.

In 1869, a game was played between Rutgers and Princeton universities,
which is considered the first American football game.

However, the rules were quite different from those played today.

In the 1870s, Canadian universities began to play their own version of
American football, based on rugby and association football (soccer).

As the game developed, Canadians introduced a series of rules that
were different from those used in the United States.

These rules included the use of a larger playing field, the introduction
of a line of scrimmage, and limiting players who could
advance over the ball (offside).

These rules were adopted by the Intercollegiate Football Association
(IFA), the organization that controlled college
American football in the United States.

In 1882, the first American football rules committee was established,
which included representatives from Canadian
and American universities.

This committee established a set of rules that closely resembled
those played today in American football.

Therefore, it can be said that Canada had a significant influence
on the development of the rules of modern American football.

9

Before rules and regulations were established for American football, players used various tactics that today would be considered illegal.

An example is players greasing themselves up with oil, but this is just one of the many illegal techniques used.

Another example is the "clothesline," which involved stretching the arm to hit the opposing player above the neck.

Hits below the waist and blindside blocks were also allowed, among other dangerous and unethical tactics.

However, as the sport developed and stricter rules were established, these illegal tactics gradually disappeared from the game.

10

American football is a very popular sport in the United States, where it is considered one of the most important sports.

According to a 2019 Gallup survey, American football is the second most popular sport in the United States, behind only basketball.

In terms of television viewership, the Super Bowl is the most-watched sporting event in the United States, often attracting over 100 million viewers.

In addition to the United States, American football also has a significant audience in Canada, where the Canadian Football League (CFL) is the main American football league.

Outside of North America, American football is less popular, although it still has fans around the world.

Some countries, such as Mexico, Japan, and Germany, have established American football leagues, while in other countries the sport is mainly played at the university or amateur level.

Despite this, American football has begun to grow in popularity in some European countries in recent years, such as in the United Kingdom, where an NFL game is held annually in London and there have been rumors of a possible expansion of the league in Europe.

Overall, American football has an audience mainly concentrated in North America, but with fans around the world and a potential to continue its international growth in the future.

11

American football is a sport that requires a large number of players to form a complete team.

In addition to the 11 players on the field, there are a large number of players on the bench who can be used in different game situations.

The size of the team can vary depending on the level of competition, geographic region, and coach's strategy.

In college football, for example, each team can have up to 85 players on their roster, while in the NFL the limit is 53 players.

Each position in American football has specific skills and characteristics that must be performed by players with the appropriate abilities.

For example, receivers must be fast and agile, while offensive linemen must be strong and able to block defenders.

The Jacksonville Jaguars, Cleveland Browns, Detroit Lions, and Houston Texans are the four teams that have never made it to a Super Bowl in the history of the NFL.

12

The Jacksonville Jaguars are a professional American football team based in Jacksonville, Florida.

They were founded in 1995 as one of the expansion teams of the NFL and have since played in the league's American Football Conference (AFC).

Despite reaching the conference finals on three occasions (1996, 1999, and 2017), they have never reached a Super Bowl.

The Cleveland Browns are a professional American football team based in Cleveland, Ohio.

They were founded in 1946 and have since played in the NFL's AFC.

The Browns won four NFL championships before the AFL-NFL merger in 1970 but have never reached a Super Bowl.

The Browns have only made the playoffs twice since their return to the NFL in 1999.

The Detroit Lions are a professional American football team based in Detroit, Michigan.

They were founded in 1930 and have since played in the NFL's NFC. Although the Lions won four NFL titles before the AFL-NFL merger in 1970, they have never reached a Super Bowl.

The Lions have won only one playoff game since their last appearance in the NFC championship game in 1991.

The Houston Texans are a professional American football team based in Houston, Texas.

They were founded in 2002 as the NFL's 32nd expansion team and have since played in the AFC.

The Texans have reached the playoffs six times but have never reached a Super Bowl.

However, the team has had success in the AFC South division, winning the division title six times.

13

An NFL game has a total duration of around 3 hours, but the effective playing time is usually much shorter.

In fact, it is estimated that there is an average of approximately 11-13 minutes of effective playing time in an NFL game.

This is due to various factors such as the breaks between plays, reviews of plays by referees, timeouts, injuries, and other factors that can stop the game clock.

Additionally, numerous commercial advertisements are aired during games, which further increases the total duration of the event.

14

The duration of the NFL (National Football League) season is 17 weeks.

It starts in September and extends until December.

During these 17 weeks, each of the 32 teams plays 16 games and has one week off.

This means that each team has one free week in which they don't play any games.

The season is divided into three parts: the regular season, playoffs, and the Super Bowl.

During the regular season, which lasts for 16 weeks, each team plays 16 games, eight at home and eight away.

The teams are divided into two conferences, the National Conference (NFC) and the American Conference (AFC), and further into four divisions each.

Teams compete within their own division and against other teams from their conference and the other conference.

After the regular season, the top six teams from each conference advance to the playoffs.

The playoffs last for three weeks and consist of three rounds of single-elimination games.

The teams that win in each round advance to the next, and the team that wins the final round from each conference face each other in the Super Bowl.

The Super Bowl is the final game of the season and is played in February.

It is one of the most-watched sporting events worldwide, and the team that wins the Super Bowl is considered the NFL champion for that year.

15

Penalties in American football are a form of discipline and regulation to ensure player safety and maintain the integrity of the game.

Referees are responsible for enforcing penalties when players commit infractions.

Regarding the use of the helmet as a weapon, the NFL has implemented new rules and sanctions to reduce the risk of serious injuries.

The rule of lowering the head to hit an opponent with the helmet is known as "spearing" and is illegal in the NFL.

Players who do so are subject to a fine and/or suspension, depending on the severity of the infraction.

Additionally, the NFL is trying to educate players on best safety practices to reduce the risk of injuries.

Besides penalties related to helmet use, there are a variety of other infractions that can result in penalties in American football.

Some examples include personal fouls such as illegal blocking, late hit, facemask grabbing, and pass interference.

There are also team infractions, such as delay of game, offside, false start, and illegal use of hands.

Penalties in American football can range from a loss of yards to ejection from the game or even a subsequent suspension.

Referees can signal an infraction by using a flag thrown on the field, indicating that a foul has been committed.

Teams can accept or decline the penalty, depending on the game situation.

16

The inaugural season of the NFL was in 1920 and featured the participation of 14 teams.

These teams included the Akron Pros, Buffalo All-Americans, Canton Bulldogs, Chicago Cardinals, Chicago Tigers, Cleveland Tigers, Columbus Panhandles, Dayton Triangles, Decatur Staleys (now Chicago Bears), Detroit Heralds, Hammond Pros, Muncie Flyers, Rochester Jeffersons, and Rock Island Independents.

Although these teams played in the NFL's inaugural season, many of them either folded or merged with other teams in the following years.

Only two teams out of the original 14 still play in the NFL today: the Decatur Staleys (now known as the Chicago Bears) and the Chicago Cardinals (now the Arizona Cardinals).

The Bears were founded in 1919 in Decatur, Illinois, as a team sponsored by a candy company called A.E. Staley Company.

In 1921, the team moved to Chicago and changed its name to the Chicago Staleys, and then to the Chicago Bears in 1922.

Throughout their history, the Bears have won nine NFL championships and one Super Bowl.

On the other hand, the Cardinals were founded in Chicago in 1898 as the Morgan Athletic Club.

In 1920, the team joined the NFL as the Chicago Cardinals. Throughout their history, the Cardinals have won two NFL championships and one Super Bowl.

In 1988, the team moved to Tempe, Arizona, and in 2006, they moved to Glendale, Arizona, where they currently play at State Farm Stadium.

17

The first televised American football game took place on October 22, 1939, and was an NFL game between the Brooklyn Dodgers and the Philadelphia Eagles at Ebbets Field in Brooklyn, New York.

The broadcast was done by NBC, and although only a few snippets of the game were shown, it is considered the first major sporting event ever to be broadcast on television.

The game broadcast was done from a television studio in New York, where cameras were strategically placed to capture the game's plays.

The signal was then broadcast live to a television receiver located at the stadium, where around 500 people were able to watch the game on a giant screen.

In those days, television was still a nascent medium, and most American homes did not yet have televisions.

Furthermore, the game broadcast was limited to the states of New York and Pennsylvania, so the audience was very limited.

Despite the technological and audience limitations of the time, the broadcast of the first American football game on television was a significant milestone in the history of the NFL and television in general.

Since then, the broadcast of sports events on television has evolved tremendously, and it is now an integral part of the sports-watching experience for millions of viewers around the world.

18

In the NFL, if two or more teams have the same record at the end of the regular season, several tiebreakers are used to determine which team advances to the playoffs or wins the division title.

If, after applying all tiebreakers, the teams are still tied, the tiebreaker is resolved by a coin toss.

The tiebreakers used in the NFL include:

-The win-loss record in games played between tied teams.

-The win-loss record in division games of tied teams.

-The win-loss record in games against teams in the same conference.

-The win-loss record in games against teams in the same conference.

-The point differential in regular season games.

-The total amount of points scored in regular season games.

-A coin toss.

The coin toss is the last tiebreaker used to determine the position of teams in the final regular season standings and in determining the teams that advance to the playoffs.

It is also used to break a tie if two or more teams are tied in their regular season record and competing for a wildcard spot in the playoffs.

The coin toss is held at a location designated by the NFL and is supervised by a league representative.

The toss is conducted between representatives of the teams involved in the tie, and the winner of the toss gets the most favorable position in the final regular season standings or advances to the playoffs.

19

The Pittsburgh Steelers were the first team to have a cheerleading squad in the 1960s.

In 1961, the owner of the Steelers, Art Rooney, wanted to find a way to improve the atmosphere at his team's games and decided to form a cheerleading squad.

However, despite being the first team to have a cheerleading squad, the Steelers decided to disband it in 1970 due to lack of interest and the need to cut costs.

Since then, they have been one of the six NFL teams that do not have a cheerleading squad, along with the Green Bay Packers, Buffalo Bills, Cleveland Browns, New York Giants, and Chicago Bears.

Despite the absence of cheerleaders on some teams, most NFL teams have a cheerleading squad that provides entertainment and animation during games.

These squads are usually made up of young women who have undergone rigorous testing and training to ensure they are physically and mentally prepared to perform in public.

In addition to cheering for the team, cheerleaders also engage in charitable activities and represent the team at community and charity events.

20

Super Bowl IV was played at a temperature of 3.9 degrees Celsius, making it the coldest Super Bowl in history.

The game was held at Tulane Stadium in New Orleans on January 11, 1970, and featured the Kansas City Chiefs and the Minnesota Vikings.

As for the date of the Super Bowl, it is true that most games have been played during the month of January.

Of the 50 editions of the Super Bowl to date, 37 have been played in January, while 13 have been played in February.

This is largely due to the fact that the NFL regular season begins in September and ends in December, which means that January is the most suitable time to celebrate the big postseason event.

It should be noted that starting with the 2001–2002 season, the NFL changed its schedule to include a bye week for each team between the end of the regular season and the start of the playoffs.

This has allowed the Super Bowl to be played later in February, which has allowed for better planning and promotion of the event.

21

In the history of the Super Bowl, the team with the lowest completion percentage is actually the Minnesota Vikings.

The Minnesota Vikings have appeared in four Super Bowls, and in those four games, they have completed only 46.8% of their passes.

This is partly due to the poor performance of quarterback Fran Tarkenton in Super Bowls VIII, IX, and XI, in which he completed only 43.8%, 44.4%, and 47.7% of his passes, respectively.

22

The Super Bowl has been played in 22 different stadiums throughout its history.

The first Super Bowl was played at the Los Angeles Memorial Coliseum in 1967, and since then it has been held at various locations throughout the United States.

The stadium that has hosted the most Super Bowls is the Superdome in New Orleans, which has been the site of seven championship games.

In addition to the Superdome, other stadiums that have hosted multiple Super Bowls are the Hard Rock Stadium in Miami (6), the Rose Bowl in Pasadena (5), the Orange Bowl in Miami (5), the Mercedes-Benz Superdome in New Orleans (7), and the University of Phoenix Stadium in Glendale, Arizona (2).

There have also been several stadiums that have hosted only one Super Bowl, including Levi's Stadium in Santa Clara, California; US Bank Stadium in Minneapolis, Minnesota; and MetLife Stadium in East Rutherford, New Jersey.

Overall, the Super Bowl has been a traveling event that has been held in cities and stadiums throughout the United States, and its location changes every year.

23

Out of the 32 teams that make up the NFL, only 19 have won the Super Bowl at least once.

Teams that have won the Super Bowl multiple times include the New England Patriots (6 victories), the Pittsburgh Steelers (6 victories), the Dallas Cowboys (5 victories), the San Francisco 49ers (5 victories), the Green Bay Packers (4 victories), the New York Giants (4 victories), the Denver Broncos (3 victories), and the Oakland Los Angeles Raiders (3 victories).

Other teams that have won the Super Bowl at least once include the Baltimore Ravens, the Tampa Bay Buccaneers, the Kansas City Chiefs, the Seattle Seahawks, the Miami Dolphins, the Washington Football Team (previously known as the Redskins), the Indianapolis Colts (previously known as the Baltimore Colts), the New York Jets, the New Orleans Saints, the Chicago Bears, and the St. Louis/Los Angeles Rams.

24

Walter Camp (1859-1925) was a prominent coach and pioneer of American football in the United States, considered by many to be the "father of American football".

Camp studied at Yale University, where he was a player and coach of the football team.

Throughout his career, he was instrumental in creating the modern rules of American football, including the line of scrimmage, the snap, and the down, among others.

Camp was also a prominent sports journalist and wrote numerous articles and essays about American football.

In addition, he was the president of the rules committee of the Intercollegiate Football Association, which allowed him to influence the development of the sport at the university level.

In recognition of his contributions to American football, Walter Camp was inducted into the College Football Hall of Fame in 1951.

Additionally, the NCAA Player of the Year Trophy is named after him.

25

The early American football games were primarily played by universities and colleges in the United States.

In the 1860s, American football was a variant of British football that was played at universities on the East Coast of the United States.

The first recorded university American football game took place in 1869 between Rutgers and Princeton Universities.

The game consisted of two teams of 25 players each, and the goal was to carry the oval ball to the opposing team's goal line.

The final score was 6-4 in favor of Rutgers.

As American football became more popular in universities, rules and norms were established for the sport.

In 1876, the Eastern Association of Football was created, which was the first regulatory body of university American football.

Throughout history, universities have played an important role in the development of American football.

In addition to being a place where players are trained, universities have been responsible for establishing the rules and norms of the sport and organizing competitions and tournaments.

Today, university American football is still very popular in the United States and is considered a talent pool for the NFL.

Many of the most prominent NFL players began their careers in university American football.

26

In the 1920s, tickets for American football games could cost around $1.

As the sport became more popular in the following decades, prices increased.

In the 1960s, for example, tickets for Super Bowl I were sold for between $6 and $12.

Nowadays, ticket prices vary widely depending on the team and the game.

For example, for Super Bowl LVI, which will be played in February 2022, ticket prices start at around $5,000 and can go up to over $30,000 for a seat in the front row.

27

The Super Bowl halftime show is a highly anticipated event and each year features a different performance often including renowned artists.

However, in the early years of the Super Bowl, the tradition was to have school and college bands perform at halftime.

The first band to perform at the Super Bowl halftime show was the Arizona State University in Super Bowl XI in 1977.

Many school and college bands performed at halftime shows in the following years.

In the 1990s, halftime performances started to change, with the appearance of artists such as Michael Jackson and Gloria Estefan.

Nowadays, halftime performances are massive events with a large production and the participation of major music stars, and have become one of the most important and anticipated moments of the Super Bowl.

28

American football players paint black lines on the upper cheekbone to reduce glare caused by sunlight or artificial light.

This glare effect can make it difficult to see and can affect the player's ability to track the movement of the ball and other players on the field.

The black paint helps reduce the contrast between the ball and the background, making visibility easier and improving the player's performance.

Additionally, some brands of paint are designed to be waterproof and sweat-resistant, meaning the paint won't run during the game.

29

William Walter "Pudge" Heffelfinger was an American football player who is considered one of the first great professional players in the history of the sport.

He was born on December 20, 1867, in Minneapolis, Minnesota and died on April 2, 1954, in Blessing, Texas.

Heffelfinger played as a guard at Yale University and was one of the most prominent players of his time.

In 1892, he accepted an offer from the Allegheny Athletic Association to play in a game against the Pittsburgh Athletic Club, becoming the first player to receive money for playing American football.

In 1893, Heffelfinger was hired by the Chicago Athletic Association to play in a game against the Chicago Colts (now known as the Chicago Bears) for a salary of $500, becoming the first professional player in the history of the NFL.

He also played for the Pittsburgh Athletic Club and the Allegheny Athletic Association.

Heffelfinger retired from American football in 1902, having been one of the most important players of his time and a pioneer in the professionalism of the sport.

In 1963, he was inducted into the Pro Football Hall of Fame in recognition of his contribution to the development of the sport.

30

In American football, "1 and 10" refers to the situation in which a team has possession of the ball and has to advance 10 yards towards the end zone to achieve a new first down and continue advancing towards the goal of scoring a touchdown.

The "1" refers to the number of the first down that the team is currently on, and the "10" refers to the number of yards they need to advance to achieve a new first down.

If the team fails to advance 10 yards in the four opportunities they have, the ball will be given to the other team.

31

Some players have scored 4 touchdowns in a single American football game.

One of the most notable is former San Francisco 49ers player Jerry Rice, who did it in Super Bowl XXIV against the Denver Broncos in 1990.

Other players who have achieved this feat in the Super Bowl include Joe Montana, Terrell Davis, and Lynn Swann.

In the regular season, the record for touchdowns in a single game is 7, set by Chicago Bears player Gale Sayers in 1965.

32

Devin Hester scored the fastest touchdown in Super Bowl history, which is the championship final of the NFL.

This touchdown occurred in Super Bowl XLI played on February 4, 2007, at Dolphin Stadium in Miami, Florida.

Devin Hester was responsible for receiving the opening kickoff and returned it to score a touchdown in just 14 seconds, which helped the Chicago Bears gain an early lead in the game.

This is the fastest touchdown in Super Bowl history and is a record that still stands.

33

The longest touchdown in NFL history
was scored by Jacoby Jones of the
Baltimore Ravens in a playoff
game in January 2013.

In that game, Jones returned a kickoff
from the Denver Broncos from the
back of his own end zone and ran
108 yards to score the touchdown.

This is the longest touchdown in NFL
history and remains the
current record.

34

In American football, a safety is a defensive play that awards two points to the defending team.

A safety occurs when a player from the offensive team is tackled in their own end zone, which means that the ball has crossed the goal line behind the offensive team's line of scrimmage.

A safety can also occur if the offensive team commits a penalty in their own end zone, or if the ball is kicked out of bounds in the end zone by a player from the offensive team.

When a safety occurs, the defending team also receives possession of the ball through a free kick.

Therefore, a safety is a very important play in American football and can have a significant impact on the game's outcome.

35

The quarterback at the waist wears a belt with small pads called "pads," which are designed to protect the player's ribs.

These pads are made of a padded and durable material that helps prevent injuries to the rib area in case of an impact.

In addition, the quarterback also typically wears a wristband or belt where he stores the team's plays and strategies, known as a "wristband."

This accessory allows the quarterback to have all the necessary information at hand to direct the team on the field.

36

There are different types of colored flags in American football, and each one has a specific use:

- **Yellow flag**: Used by referees to signal a penalty in the game. When a yellow flag is thrown, it means a penalty has been observed, and the game is stopped for the referees to discuss and decide on what action to take.

- **White flag**: Used to signal a timeout in the game. When a white flag is thrown, the clock stops, and players have a brief break.

- **Red flag**: Used to signal unsportsmanlike or violent conduct. When a red flag is thrown, the responsible player can be penalized or even ejected from the game.

- **Blue flag**: Used by referees to signal a pass interference penalty. When a blue flag is thrown, it means a defender has interfered with the receiver in a pass play, resulting in a penalty.

- **Green flag**: Used to signal a player has gone out of bounds. When a green flag is thrown, the game is stopped, and it is determined whether the player can return to the field or not.

- **Orange flag**: Used by the head referee to signal an illegal out of bounds penalty in a pass play. When an orange flag is thrown, it means an offensive player has gone out of bounds before catching the ball in a pass play.

- **Black flag**: Used to signal an illegal substitution penalty. When a black flag is thrown, it means a player has entered or exited the field illegally and can be penalized. It is important to note that while these are some of the most common colored flags, they may vary depending on the league or level of competition and the specific rules of the game.

37

The longest pass in the history of American football is a 99-yard touchdown pass thrown by Dallas Cowboys quarterback Tony Romo to his receiver Sam Hurd in a game against the Seattle Seahawks in October 2006.

The pass started at the Cowboys' 1-yard line, and Hurd caught it at the Seahawks' 40-yard line before running it into the end zone.

This is the longest pass in NFL history and still stands as the current record.

38

The longest Super Bowl in history was Super Bowl LI in 2017, in which the New England Patriots faced off against the Atlanta Falcons.

The game lasted a total of 4 hours and 14 minutes, including a 15-minute overtime period that was played for the first time in a Super Bowl.

The Patriots won the game 34-28 after coming back from a 25-point deficit in the second half, making it one of the most exciting games in Super Bowl history.

39

Tom Brady is widely considered one of the greatest players in the history of American football.

Born in California in 1977, Brady played college football at the University of Michigan before being selected by the New England Patriots in the sixth round of the NFL Draft in 2000.

Despite his late selection in the draft, Brady quickly proved to be a talented player and became the starting quarterback for the Patriots in his second season in the NFL. In 2002, he led the Patriots to their first Super Bowl title in franchise history.

Brady continued to have success throughout his career, leading the Patriots to a total of nine Super Bowl appearances and winning six titles.

In 2020, Brady left the Patriots and signed with the Tampa Bay Buccaneers, where he won his seventh Super Bowl title in the 2020-2021 season.

In addition to his success in the Super Bowl, Brady has been selected to the Pro Bowl 14 times and has been named the NFL's Most Valuable Player three times.

40

Doug Williams is a former NFL quarterback who played for several teams throughout his career, including the Washington Football Team and the Tampa Bay Buccaneers.

However, he is best known for his performance in Super Bowl XXII in 1988, where he set the record for most touchdown passes in a single quarter with 4 scores in the second quarter of the game.

Williams led the Washington Football Team to an impressive 42-10 victory over the Denver Broncos in that game, earning the Super Bowl Most Valuable Player award.

He was the first African American quarterback to win a Super Bowl, and his performance is still remembered as one of the best in the history of the game.

After his playing career, Williams went on to become a coach at various universities and professional teams.

He also served as an executive in the NFL, working for the Tampa Bay Buccaneers and the Washington Football Team in high-level positions.

41

**Being a good free safety in American football requires
a combination of physical and mental skills.**

Here are some tips to improve in this position:

-Learn the defensive system: It is important to understand the strategy and responsibilities of the defensive system in order to make the best decisions on the field. This will also help communicate better with the rest of the defensive team.

-Study opponents: Analyze opponents' playing styles in order to anticipate their moves and react effectively on the field.

-Improve your speed and agility: Free safeties need to have good speed and agility to cover a large amount of ground on the field and defend against receivers.

-Work on your tackling technique: Free safeties often have to make tackles in open spaces, which can be a challenge. Make sure to have good tackling technique to make effective stops.

-Develop your coverage skills: The ability to cover receivers is essential for a free safety. Practice coverage techniques and improve your game-reading ability to make the necessary interceptions and defenses.

-Be a leader on the field: Free safeties often have to make quick decisions and lead the defense on the field. Develop your leadership skills to motivate the team and make effective decisions.

42

It is difficult to determine who the best safety in NFL history is as there have been many outstanding players in this position.

However, there are some names that are highly recognized in the history of American football.

One of the most prominent players is Ronnie Lott, who played for the San Francisco 49ers, Los Angeles Raiders, and New York Jets in his 14-year career.

Lott was selected for 10 Pro Bowls, won four Super Bowls, and was inducted into the Pro Football Hall of Fame in 2000.

Another highly distinguished player is Ed Reed, who played for the Baltimore Ravens and Houston Texans in his 12-year career.

Reed was selected for nine Pro Bowls, won a Super Bowl, and was named Defensive Player of the Year in 2004.

Reed also leads the NFL in career regular season and playoff interceptions combined, with a total of 64.

Other outstanding players in the safety position include Paul Krause, Ken Houston, Brian Dawkins, and Troy Polamalu, among others.

All of these players have left a great impact on NFL history and are considered some of the best safeties of all time.

43

Kamara is the nickname of American football player Alvin Kamara, a running back who currently plays for the New Orleans Saints of the NFL.

Kamara was born in Georgia in 1995 and played football at the University of Tennessee before being selected by the Saints in the third round of the 2017 NFL Draft.

Since arriving in the league, Kamara has been one of the top emerging stars in the NFL.

In his rookie season, Kamara led the league in average yards per carry and received the NFL Offensive Rookie of the Year award.

Since then, he has been selected three times for the Pro Bowl and has been named First-team All-Pro twice.

Kamara is known for his ability as a runner and receiver, making him a threat in all offensive situations.

He is also recognized for his distinctive hair style, which includes colorful braids and unique designs.

Off the field, Kamara is known for his unique personality and love for culture and fashion.

He is also an avid fan of professional wrestling and has appeared in several WWE events.

44

The most successful team in the history of professional American football is the Pittsburgh Steelers, with a total of 6 Super Bowl titles.

The Steelers have appeared in a total of 8 Super Bowls and have won the championship in the seasons of 1974, 1975, 1978, 1979, 2005, and 2008.

In addition, they have won a total of 23 division titles, 8 conference championships, and have made 32 playoff appearances in their history.

It is important to mention that the Pittsburgh Steelers are one of the oldest teams in the NFL, as they were founded in 1933.

Throughout their history, they have had great players and coaches, such as the legendary coach Chuck Noll and players like Terry Bradshaw, Franco Harris, Lynn Swann, Jack Lambert, and Mean Joe Greene, among others.

The Steelers are known for having one of the strongest defenses in the history of the NFL, and their strategy of hard and aggressive play has allowed them to remain one of the most successful teams in the league.

45

There are several factors that can influence the distance that a football can be thrown in American football, including throwing technique, arm strength, and the speed of the run-up before throwing.

Here are some tips for throwing further in American football:

-Improve throwing technique: To throw further, it is important to have proper throwing technique. This involves having a solid stance, good throwing mechanics, and proper follow-through during the throw. It is recommended to work with a coach or use online training videos to improve throwing technique.

-Strengthen the arm: To throw further, it is important to have a strong arm. Specific strength training exercises for the arm can be done, such as push-ups, weight lifting, and resistance band training.

-Improve speed: The speed of the run-up before throwing can have an impact on the throwing distance. To increase speed, speed and agility training exercises can be done, such as sprints and jumping exercises.

-Use the body: To throw further, it is important to use the entire body in the throw. This involves not only the arm, but also the legs and torso. Make sure to be balanced and transfer the energy from your body to the ball during the throw.

-Practice: Practice is essential to improve throwing distance. Practice regularly and work on improving technique and strength to throw further.

46

The NFL contributes an approximate amount of $5,000 per ring and is responsible for the creation and design of the rings.

However, the total cost of Super Bowl rings is covered by the winning franchise.

The value of each ring varies depending on the design and materials used, but it is estimated that the average cost of a Super Bowl ring is around $30,000.

However, some teams have spent much more on their Super Bowl rings, even surpassing $100,000 per ring.

47

The cost of a commercial during the Super Bowl broadcast varies from year to year and is considered one of the most expensive advertising spaces in the world.

For the 2023 Super Bowl, the cost of a 30-second ad is estimated to be $7 million.

The cost of advertising during the Super Bowl has increased over the years due to the large number of viewers who tune in to the event.

On average, it is estimated that around 100 million people watch the Super Bowl each year in the United States.

Advertising during the Super Bowl is highly valued by companies, as it is a unique opportunity to reach a massive audience and capture the public's attention.

48

The player who currently holds the record for the most touchdowns in NFL history is Jerry Rice, who registered a total of 208 touchdowns in his career.

Rice played as a wide receiver for the San Francisco 49ers, Oakland Raiders, and Seattle Seahawks during his NFL career, which spanned from 1985 to 2004.

He is considered one of the greatest players in the history of American football and was inducted into the NFL Hall of Fame in 2010.

49

Devin Hester is considered one of the greatest returners in NFL history.

During his career in the league, Hester set several records in kick returns and was named to the Pro Bowl three times.

In addition to his fastest touchdown in Super Bowl XLI, Hester also holds the record for the most kick returns for touchdowns in NFL history, with a total of 20.

After his NFL career, Hester was inducted into the University of Miami Hall of Fame in 2018.

50

The game with the fewest points in NFL history was played on November 10, 1940 between the teams of the Detroit Lions and the Chicago Cardinals.

The final score of the game was 0-0, making it the only game in NFL history in which neither team scored any points.

It is important to note that at that time the league did not have overtime in case of a tie, so the game ended in a tie.

Since then, there have been several games with low scores, but none have matched the record of that 1940 game.

51

Ladainian Tomlinson, former player for the San Diego Chargers and New York Jets, is the player who holds the record for the most touchdowns in a regular season of the NFL, with a total of 31 touchdowns.

This impressive record was set during the 2006 season, in which Tomlinson recorded 28 rushing touchdowns and 3 receiving touchdowns, in addition to the extra points and field goals converted.

This achievement made Tomlinson the Most Valuable Player (MVP) of the NFL for the 2006 season and secured his position as one of the greatest running backs of all time.

Tomlinson's record surpassed the previous mark set by former Seattle Seahawks player Shaun Alexander, who scored 28 touchdowns in the 2005 season.

It is important to note that although Tomlinson's record was set in a regular season, there are other players who have scored more touchdowns in a single season, including postseason.

For example, Jerry Rice scored 38 touchdowns in a season in 1987, but only 23 of them were in the regular season, while the other 15 were in playoffs.

52

What do American football players shout?

One of the most commonly used phrases by quarterbacks is "White Eighty," which some viewers may mistake for the pronunciation of the number 180 in English (one-eighty).

Quarterbacks shout it with a certain cadence to indicate to the center that they are ready to begin the play.

In addition to "White Eighty," players use a variety of shouts and signals to communicate on the field.

These shouts, also known as "audible changes," are used to change the original play that was planned in response to the opposing team's defense.

Other examples of audible changes include "Omaha," which was popularized by former Denver Broncos quarterback Peyton Manning and is used to indicate that the play will be executed on the opposite side of the field.

Another example is "Hut Hut Hike," which is commonly used by quarterbacks to indicate when the center should snap the ball to them to begin the play.

In addition to these shouts, players also use hand signals and movements to communicate.

For example, a receiver may indicate that they will run a specific route by raising their hand in the air or moving their head in a certain direction.

Offensive linemen can also point to others to indicate who should block whom on a specific play.

53

The National Football League (NFL) and the National Athletic Trainers' Association (NATA) recommend that football helmets be replaced at least every ten years from the date of manufacture.

This is because the material used to make helmets, such as foam and plastic, deteriorates over time and may lose its ability to adequately protect the player against head injuries.

Additionally, helmets should be regularly inspected for any damage or wear and replaced if necessary.

54

Super Bowl LI (51) between the New England Patriots and Atlanta Falcons, played on February 5, 2017, is considered the longest Super Bowl in NFL history.

The game had a total duration of 4 hours and 51 minutes, including overtime.

The Patriots achieved a historic comeback after trailing 28-3 in the third quarter, managing to tie the game in the final seconds of regulation time and winning in overtime with a touchdown by James White.

Super Bowl LI is remembered as one of the most exciting and spectacular games in league history.

55

In the NFL, the distance that a quarterback can throw the ball varies depending on several factors, such as the QB's skill, the offensive line protection, the quality of the receivers, among others.

On average, a QB can throw the ball between 50 and 60 yards in the air, which is equivalent to a distance of 45 to 55 meters.

However, some quarterbacks with exceptional skills can throw the ball beyond 70 yards.

It's important to mention that throwing is not only about throwing the ball far, but also about throwing it accurately and in the right place so that the receiver can catch it and advance.

56

The term "Super Bowl" originated from the idea of the owner of the Kansas City Chiefs, Lamar Hunt, who was looking for an attractive way to call the championship game of the newly created AFL (American Football League) and would face the winner of the NFL (National Football League) championship.

Hunt was inspired by his son's game called "Super Ball" and decided to change the last word to "Bowl," which also referred to the bowls used in college football games.

Since then, the term "Super Bowl" has become synonymous with the NFL championship game, and it is one of the most important and watched sports events worldwide.

57

The speed of a football player can vary depending on their position and skills.

In general, the fastest players are the wide receivers and cornerbacks, who can run the 40-yard dash in less than 4.4 seconds.

As for the maximum speed, it has been recorded that some players reach speeds of up to 35 km/h (21.7 mph) during a game.

However, most players run at an average speed of around 20 km/h (12.4 mph) during games.

It's important to highlight that speed is not the only important skill in football.

Strength, agility, endurance, and the ability to change direction quickly are also essential skills in this sport.

58

The game with the most points in NFL history was played between the Washington Redskins and the New York Giants in 1966.

In this game, both teams scored a total of 113 points, with a final score of 72-41 in favor of the Redskins.

This game is considered one of the most exciting in NFL history, as both teams set several offensive records during the game.

The Redskins set an NFL record with 72 points scored in a single game, while the Giants set a record with 41 points scored in the second half of the game.

This game remains remembered as one of the most exciting and offensive in NFL history.

59

The weight of a football player's uniform can vary depending on the position and team.

In general, the full uniform can weigh around 4.5 to 5.5 kilograms (10-12 pounds).

The helmet, which is one of the heaviest components of the uniform, can weigh around 1.3 kilograms (3 pounds) or more.

Shoulder pads can weigh around 1.4 to 2.3 kilograms (3-5 pounds), while the jersey and pants can weigh around 0.9 to 1.8 kilograms (2-4 pounds) in total.

In addition, players may also wear neck protectors, rib protectors, gloves, elbow pads, and knee pads, which also add weight to the uniform.

60

Some football players receive Toradol injections before games to help relieve pain and reduce inflammation in the body.

However, the use of this medication has also been criticized due to its side effects, which can include gastrointestinal problems, bleeding, and kidney problems.

Additionally, some players have reported receiving injections without being fully informed about the associated risks.

The National Football League (NFL) has taken steps to limit the use of Toradol, requiring teams to report on its use and limiting the number of injections that can be administered to players in a single game or week.

61

The prices of American football helmets vary widely depending on the brand, model, and level of protection.

Generally, technologically advanced helmets that offer greater protection are more expensive.

In the specialized sports equipment market, American football helmets can range in price from $50 to $500.

Additionally, professional and college teams may have agreements with helmet manufacturers to obtain discounts on bulk purchases.

62

How does Tom Brady eat?

The Tom Brady diet has a lot in common with the Mediterranean diet, which studies consistently link to improved heart health.

Both include lots of fruits, vegetables, whole grains, legumes, olive oil, nuts, and seeds, as well as limited amounts of lean meats and fish.

It also eliminates some foods considered "inflammatory," such as dairy, refined flour, refined sugar, caffeine, and alcohol.

Instead, it focuses on fresh, unprocessed foods, avoiding packaged and processed foods.

Brady has also spoken about the importance of drinking plenty of water and maintaining good hydration overall.

Brady is known for being very careful about his diet and lifestyle, and has attributed his longevity in the NFL to these factors.

63

Emmitt Smith is a former American football player who played as a running back during his career in the NFL.

He is the all-time leader in rushing yards in NFL history, with a total of 18,355 yards in his career.

Smith played for the Dallas Cowboys and the Arizona Cardinals, and was selected to eight Pro Bowls and chosen three times as the NFL Offensive Player of the Year.

He also won three Super Bowls with the Cowboys.

64

The American football player considered to be the fastest is Tyreek Hill, a wide receiver for the Kansas City Chiefs of the National Football League (NFL).

Hill is known for his impressive speed, which has allowed him to excel in his position as a receiver.

In 2016, during speed tests at the Scouting Combine (an event where college players are evaluated by NFL teams), Hill recorded a time of 4.29 seconds in the 40-yard dash (36.6 meters), making him one of the fastest players in the history of the event.

In addition to his speed, Hill is also known for his ability to change direction quickly and his skill in running with the ball after the catch, making him a very dangerous player on the field.

It is important to note that there are other American football players who also excel in speed, such as Marquise Goodwin (wide receiver for the Chicago Bears), John Ross (wide receiver for the New York Giants), and Henry Ruggs III (wide receiver for the Las Vegas Raiders), among others.

65

The height that an American football player can jump varies according to various factors, such as the position they play, their height, weight, training, and genetics.

On average, an American football player can jump between 75 and 90 centimeters in a vertical jump.

However, some players can exceed this mark, especially those who play in positions that require higher jumps, such as receivers or defenders who must jump to intercept a pass.

Additionally, some players may specifically train to improve their jumping ability, which can allow them to exceed the average mark.

Jump training exercises include squats, box jumps, long jumps, and one-legged jumps.

66

The lightest player in the NFL can vary from season to season, as teams constantly make acquisitions and cuts.

However, the lightest player in the NFL in the 2020 season was Gunner Olszewski, a wide receiver and specialist in special teams for the New England Patriots, weighing 77 kilograms.

Olszewski, who is 1.75 meters tall, is known for his speed and ability to return kicks and punts on the Patriots' special teams.

Despite his relatively low weight, he has proven to be a valuable player for the team and has scored several touchdowns in his NFL career.

It is important to note that, in general, American football players tend to have a robust physical build and a high weight, due to the physical demands of the sport.

However, skill and talent are more important than weight or height in the NFL.

67

The heaviest player in NFL history is Aaron Gibson, who played in the league from 1999 to 2004.

Gibson, who was an offensive tackle, reached a weight of 215 kilograms during his NFL career.

Gibson played for several teams throughout his career, including the Detroit Lions, Chicago Bears, and Dallas Cowboys.

Despite his impressive size, Gibson failed to have a successful career in the NFL and was criticized for his lack of fitness and tendency to sustain injuries.

Since then, the NFL has implemented measures to ensure that players maintain a healthy weight and physical fitness to prevent injuries and improve their performance on the field.

68

Regarding the ideal height for a quarterback in the NFL, there is no exact measure established, however, most successful quarterbacks in the league have a height ranging between 1.85 and 1.98 meters.

A height of at least 1.85 meters is considered important for a quarterback because it allows them to have a better view of the field and a wider perspective over the offensive line.

This allows them to see the available play options and make quicker and more effective decisions.

Additionally, a taller height can also be beneficial for quarterbacks as it allows them to have a greater wingspan and wider throwing range, enabling them to throw the ball over defenders and avoid being blocked.

However, there are exceptions to this rule, as some quarterbacks have succeeded in the NFL despite having a height below average.

For example, Russell Wilson of the Seattle Seahawks, who measures 1.80 meters, has been one of the most successful quarterbacks in the league in recent years.

The most important thing for a quarterback in the NFL is to have the necessary skills, intelligence, and accuracy to lead their team and win games.

69

The Dallas Cowboys are considered the most popular team in the NFL.

The popularity of the Cowboys is largely due to their history of success in the league, as they have won five Super Bowls and have a long list of legendary players on their roster.

Additionally, the Cowboys have built a very powerful brand over the years, thanks to their iconic logo and famous nickname, "America's Team".

This has helped attract a very broad and diverse fan base across the country, including many fans who have no geographical connection to Dallas or Texas.

According to surveys and market studies, the Cowboys are consistently one of the most popular teams in the United States and internationally.

They are also known for having one of the best attendances in home games, with the AT&T Stadium, their stadium, being one of the largest and most modern in the NFL.

It should be noted that other teams also have a large fan base in the NFL, including the Pittsburgh Steelers, Green Bay Packers, New England Patriots, and San Francisco 49ers, among others.

The popularity of a team can vary depending on various factors, such as their history of success, geographical location, brand, and playing style.

70

To become an NFL player, a combination of physical, mental, and emotional skills is required.

Here are some requirements and recommendations that could help someone become an NFL player:

-Physical ability: NFL players must have a combination of speed, strength, endurance, agility, and coordination to compete at the highest level. This requires a commitment to consistent physical training and a healthy diet.

-Technical ability: In addition to physical ability, NFL players must be experts in the specific skills and techniques of their position. This requires rigorous training and practice in game techniques and strategies.

-Previous experience: Most NFL players have previous experience in football, either in high school or college. It is important to be successful at these levels before considering playing in the NFL.

-Education: The NFL values education and intelligence in its players. Players must have the ability to read and understand plays, and communicate effectively with their teammates and coaches.

-Commitment and perseverance: The path to becoming an NFL player is not easy, and requires a great deal of commitment and perseverance. Players must be willing to work hard and overcome obstacles to achieve their goal.

Additionally, the NFL offers a variety of programs and opportunities to help young players develop their skills and improve their chances of success. These programs include recruitment events, specialized training, and career advice.

71

The tallest quarterback in NFL history is Dan McGwire, who played for the Seattle Seahawks and Miami Dolphins in the 1990s.

McGwire measured 2.03 meters (6 feet 8 inches).

However, currently, the tallest quarterback in the NFL is Brock Osweiler, who is also 2.03 meters tall and has played for several teams, including the Denver Broncos and the Miami Dolphins.

Another notably tall quarterback in the NFL is Jacksonville Jaguars rookie Jake Luton, who also measures 2.03 meters.

72

The most important position in American football varies depending on each team and coach's perspective, as each position has a crucial role in the team's success.

However, there are some positions that are generally considered more important due to their role in the game:

- **Quarterback:** This is the most well-known and recognized position in American football. The quarterback is the team leader and is responsible for directing the offense. They must have exceptional throwing and reading defenses skills, as well as the ability to make quick decisions on the field.

- **Offensive line:** The offensive line is crucial in protecting the quarterback and opening up holes for runners. Members of the offensive line must be strong, agile, and have great coordination to work together and protect the quarterback.

- **Defensive line:** The defensive line is responsible for stopping the opposing team's offense and pressuring the quarterback. Members of the defensive line must be strong, fast, and have great skill in reading the opposing team's plays.

- **Safety:** Safeties are the final defenders on the field and are responsible for stopping long pass plays and runs. They must have great speed, coverage ability, and strength to stop runners.

- **Kicker:** The kicker is important because they have the responsibility of scoring extra points and field goals. They must have great accuracy and strength in their kicks.

73

The choice of the best American football ball brand can vary depending on the preference of each player or team, but there are some brands that have consistently been well-regarded in the NFL and other levels of the sport.

Among the most popular brands are Wilson, Nike, and Adidas.

Wilson is one of the most popular and recognized American football ball brands.

Wilson manufactures the official NFL footballs and is known for their quality and durability.

Wilson balls typically have a synthetic leather cover and a cotton thread lining to improve grip and stability in the air.

Nike is another popular brand that produces high-quality American football balls.

Nike balls typically have a synthetic leather cover and a polyester or foam lining to improve durability and grip.

Nike balls also tend to have eye-catching designs and bright colors to increase visibility on the field.

Adidas has also started producing American football balls and has been well-regarded for their quality and durability.

Adidas balls typically have a synthetic leather cover and a cotton thread lining to improve grip and stability in the air.

74

The NFL has strict regulations on the inflation of American footballs. According to current rules, balls must be inflated between 12.5 and 13.5 pounds per square inch (psi).

Additionally, the ball must be checked by a referee before each game to ensure it meets the proper inflation requirements.

Proper inflation of an American football is important because it affects how the ball moves through the air and how it is handled.

If the ball is overinflated, it will be harder to grip and catch, and may also bounce unpredictably.

If the ball is underinflated, it will be easier to grip and catch, but it will also be harder to throw accurately and with speed.

It is important to note that regulation of American football inflation has been controversial in the past, especially in the case known as "Deflategate" in 2015, in which the New England Patriots were accused of illegally deflating balls during an AFC championship game.

Since then, the NFL has taken additional measures to ensure proper ball inflation regulations are met.

75

One of the shortest players in NFL history is former Kansas City Chiefs running back Darren Sproles, who measured 1.65 meters.

Despite his height, Sproles had a successful career in the NFL, playing for 14 seasons and achieving over 19,000 career yards, being considered one of the best kick return and pass-catching specialists.

Another notably short player in the NFL is New England Patriots receiver J.J. Taylor, who measures 1.68 meters.

Although small in stature, Taylor is a fast and agile player who has proven to be a valuable asset on the field.

76

The most expensive stadium in the United States is the SoFi Stadium in Inglewood, California, home of the American football teams Los Angeles Rams and Los Angeles Chargers.

The stadium was opened in 2020 with a construction cost of around $5.5 billion, making it the most expensive stadium not only in the United States but in the whole world.

The SoFi Stadium is a modern and luxurious stadium with a capacity of over 70,000 spectators, and features a wide range of amenities and advanced technologies to enhance the fan experience during games.

77

The cost of a box seat in a stadium varies depending on many factors, such as the team, the location of the box, the size of the box, the season, etc.

In general, prices can range from a few thousand dollars per season to several hundred thousand or even millions of dollars for a luxury box in a top-tier stadium.

For example, at the Dallas Cowboys' AT&T Stadium, box seat prices range from $25,000 to $500,000 or more per season.

78

American football players perform a variety of exercises to improve their strength, speed, agility, and endurance.

Some of the most common exercises include:

-Weightlifting: American football players often perform weightlifting exercises, such as squats, bench presses, deadlifts, bicep curls, and military presses, to improve their strength and power.

-Speed and agility training: American football players perform speed and agility exercises, such as sprint runs, directional change exercises, jumps, and box jumps, to improve their speed, coordination, and responsiveness.

-Cardiovascular training: American football players also perform cardiovascular exercises to improve their endurance and lung capacity, such as running, swimming, cycling, and circuit training.

-Flexibility exercises: American football players perform stretching exercises to improve their flexibility and reduce the risk of injuries.

-Specific skill training: American football players also practice specific exercises for their position, such as throwing and catching passes, blocking and tackling, to improve their skills on the field.

79

Patrick Mahomes II, also known as Pat Mahomes, is an American football quarterback who currently plays in the National Football League (NFL) for the Kansas City Chiefs.

He was born on September 17, 1995, in Tyler, Texas, and is the son of former Major League Baseball pitcher Pat Mahomes.

Mahomes played college football at Texas Tech, where he stood out as one of the top quarterbacks in the NCAA.

He was selected in the first round of the 2017 NFL Draft by the Kansas City Chiefs, and in his second season in the league in 2018, he became the NFL MVP (Most Valuable Player) and led the Chiefs to the Super Bowl, where they lost to the New England Patriots.

In the 2019 season, Mahomes led the Chiefs to their first NFL championship in 50 years, winning the Super Bowl MVP award.

He was also named the NFL Offensive Player of the Year that season.

Mahomes is known for his ability to throw incredible and accurate passes from unorthodox angles and positions, as well as his ability to read the defense and make creative plays on the field.

He is considered one of the best quarterbacks in the NFL today, and many see him as a future member of the Pro Football Hall of Fame.

In addition to his football career, Mahomes is also known for his charitable work through his 15 and the Mahomies Foundation, which supports charitable organizations focused on education, children's health, and sports safety in underserved communities.

80

Terry Bradshaw is a retired American football player who played as a quarterback in the National Football League (NFL) for the Pittsburgh Steelers from 1970 to 1983.

He was born on September 2, 1948, in Shreveport, Louisiana, and is known as one of the best quarterbacks in the history of the NFL.

Bradshaw was selected in the first round of the 1970 NFL Draft by the Pittsburgh Steelers, and quickly became a leader and star of the team.

During his 14-year career with the Steelers, he won four Super Bowls (IX, X, XIII, and XIV), was named MVP of two Super Bowls, and was selected to the Pro Bowl three times.

Bradshaw is remembered for his strong arm and his ability to throw deep and accurate passes.

He was also known for his ability to lead and motivate his team, and for his ability to make important plays in critical moments of the game.

After retiring from football in 1983, Bradshaw became a successful and popular sports commentator on television, and has worked for several networks, including CBS, Fox, and NBC.

He has also had a career in country music and has acted in several movies and television shows.

Bradshaw was inducted into the Pro Football Hall of Fame in 1989, and has been recognized as one of the greatest quarterbacks of all time.

81

Joe Montana is a former American football player who played as a quarterback in the National Football League (NFL) for the San Francisco 49ers and Kansas City Chiefs from 1979 to 1994.

He was born on June 11, 1956 in New Eagle, Pennsylvania, and is considered one of the best quarterbacks in the history of the NFL.

Montana was selected in the third round of the 1979 NFL Draft by the San Francisco 49ers, and quickly became a leader and star of the team.

During his 16-year career in the NFL, he won four Super Bowls (XVI, XIX, XXIII, and XXIV) and was named MVP of three Super Bowls.

He was also selected to the Pro Bowl eight times and was named NFL Offensive Player of the Year twice.

Montana is remembered for his ability to make important plays in critical moments of the game, and for his ability to read the defense and throw accurate passes.

He was also known for his ability to improvise and make plays with his feet, as well as his leadership and ability to motivate his team.

After retiring from football in 1995, Montana became a successful entrepreneur and has been involved in several companies, including a winery and a technology company.

He has also been a television commentator and has worked on various sports programs.

Montana was inducted into the Pro Football Hall of Fame in 2000, and is considered one of the greatest quarterbacks of all time.

In summary, Joe Montana is an American football legend who has left a lasting legacy in the NFL and in popular culture.

82

Troy Aikman is a former American football player who played as a quarterback in the National Football League (NFL) for the Dallas Cowboys from 1989 to 2000.

He was born on November 21, 1966 in West Covina, California, and is considered one of the best quarterbacks in the history of the NFL.

Aikman was selected in the first round of the 1989 NFL Draft by the Dallas Cowboys, and quickly became a leader and star of the team.

During his 12-year career in the NFL, he won three Super Bowls (XXVII, XXVIII, and XXX) and was named MVP of Super Bowl XXVII.

He was also selected to the Pro Bowl six times and was named NFL Offensive Player of the Year in 1992.

Aikman is remembered for his ability to read the defense and throw accurate passes, as well as his leadership and ability to motivate his team.

He was also known for his ability to make important plays in critical moments of the game.

After retiring from football in 2001, Aikman became a successful television commentator and has worked for various networks, including Fox and CBS.

He has also been a successful entrepreneur and has been involved in several companies, including a chain of restaurants.

Aikman was inducted into the Pro Football Hall of Fame in 2006, and is considered one of the greatest quarterbacks of all time.

83

The American football player who has earned the most money in his career is quarterback Drew Brees.

According to Forbes' list of the world's highest-paid athletes in 2020, Brees had earned a total of $269.7 million dollars during his career in the NFL up to that point.

Brees played for the San Diego Chargers and the New Orleans Saints during his 20-year career in the NFL, and won a Super Bowl with the Saints in 2010.

In addition to his player salary, Brees has also had endorsement deals with companies such as Nike, PepsiCo, Wrangler, and Xbox, among others.

84

Brett Favre is a former American football player who played as a quarterback in the NFL for 20 seasons, mainly for the Green Bay Packers.

Favre is considered one of the greatest quarterbacks of all time, having won three NFL Most Valuable Player awards and leading the Packers to two Super Bowls, winning one of them.

Among Favre's peculiarities is the fact that he supposedly wore the same socks and pants throughout the season.

This practice has been mentioned in various articles and interviews throughout his career, although it is not known for certain whether it was true or not.

While it may seem strange to wear the same clothes throughout the season, it is common for athletes to have certain routines and superstitions that help them feel comfortable and prepared to compete.

In Favre's case, if he really did wear the same clothes, he may have done so to have a constant and familiar feeling on the field, which would allow him to focus on the game instead of his attire.

85

Brian Urlacher is a former American football player who played as a linebacker for the Chicago Bears for 13 seasons in the NFL.

Urlacher is considered one of the greatest linebackers of all time, having been selected to the Pro Bowl eight times and named NFL Defensive Player of the Year in 2005.

As for his habit of eating two chicken sandwiches before each game, it has been mentioned in several interviews and articles throughout his career.

According to reports, Urlacher had a very specific routine before games, which included eating these chicken sandwiches.

86

Ray Lewis.

He is a retired American football player who played as
a linebacker for the Baltimore Ravens for
17 seasons in the NFL.

Lewis is considered one of the best linebackers in history,
having been selected to the Pro Bowl 13 times and
named NFL Defensive Player of the Year twice.

As for his practices before games, it is known that Lewis
had a very specific routine that included praying
on the field and stretching.

According to reports, Lewis used to pray on the field
before every game, often with other teammates.

He also had a stretching routine that he performed
before the team warm-up, which included specific
movements and poses.

For Lewis, these practices were important not only for
his physical preparation but also for his mental
and spiritual well-being.

Prayer and meditation are common among many athletes
as a way to maintain focus and calmness before a game,
and can help reduce stress and anxiety.

87

Deion Sanders.

He is a retired American football player who played as a cornerback for several NFL teams, including the San Francisco 49ers.

Sanders is considered one of the best cornerbacks in history, having been selected to the Pro Bowl eight times and twice won the NFL Defensive Player of the Year award.

Before each game, Sanders would listen to the same song: "I Feel Good" by James Brown.

This ritual may have been a way for Sanders to mentally prepare for the game and increase his confidence.

Sanders was also known for his aggressive playing style and speed.

As a cornerback, Sanders was able to effectively cover opposing receivers and was also an outstanding special teams player.

After his NFL career, Sanders became a sports television analyst and also ventured into music and entertainment.

His legacy in American football continues to be an inspiration to many young players and sports fans.

88

Jerome Bettis is a former American football player who played as a running back for the Pittsburgh Steelers for 10 seasons in the NFL.

Bettis is known for being one of the best runners in history, having been selected for the Pro Bowl six times and winning a Super Bowl with the Steelers in 2006.

Bettis had a very particular ritual before each game, which included taking a nap.

Bettis believed that a 20 to 30-minute nap before the game helped him relax and stay alert during the game.

Many athletes have relaxation rituals before games to help reduce stress and anxiety and improve their concentration.

Bettis was also known for his physical and powerful playing style.

As a running back, Bettis was able to break tackles and gain yards after contact, which made him a highly respected player by his teammates and opponents.

After his NFL career, Bettis became a sports television analyst and also became involved in various businesses and charitable causes.

89

Terrell Owens is a former American football player who played as a receiver for several NFL teams, including the San Francisco 49ers.

Owens is considered one of the best receivers in history, having been selected for the Pro Bowl 6 times and leading the league in receptions twice.

Owens reportedly had a particular ritual before each game that involved wearing shorts under his football pants.

Owens believed that wearing shorts gave him a sense of security and comfort on the field.

Owens was also known for his aggressive playing style and his ability to catch difficult passes.

As a receiver, Owens was able to make big plays and gain yards after the catch, which made him a valuable player for his teams.

After his NFL career, Owens became a sports television analyst and also participated in several reality shows.

90

John Henderson is a former American football player who played as a defensive tackle for the Jacksonville Jaguars for several seasons in the NFL.

Henderson is known for being a physically dominant player on the field, with an impressive height and weight that made him intimidating to his opponents.

Henderson had a particular ritual before each game that involved receiving a strong slap on the chest from one of his teammates.

The slap was so hard that it sometimes left a mark on Henderson's chest, but he believed that it helped him mentally prepare for the game.

Henderson was also known for his physical and powerful playing style on the field.

As a defensive tackle, Henderson was able to control the line of scrimmage and stop opposing runners and quarterbacks.

After his NFL career, Henderson became a football coach and also became involved in various charitable causes.

91

Randy Moss.

He is a former American football player who played as a
wide receiver in the NFL for several teams, including
the Minnesota Vikings.

Moss is considered one of the greatest receivers of all time due
to his ability to run precise routes, catch difficult passes,
and make spectacular plays.

Reportedly, Moss had a unique ritual before games where
he would cut his hair in the shape of a crescent moon.

The crescent moon was cut into the top of his head,
right at the hairline.

Moss often used different designs for his haircuts,
but always included the crescent moon.

Moss was also known for his exciting playing style and
charismatic personality.

He was selected to the Pro Bowl six times and was
named first-team All-Pro four times.

He also set several NFL records, including the record for
most receiving touchdowns in a season (23).

Moss retired from the NFL in 2012 after a 14-year career.

Since then, he has worked as a football analyst for various media
outlets and has been inducted into the Professional Football Hall
of Fame in recognition of his achievements on the field.

92

Jerry Rice.

He is considered by many to be the greatest receiver of all time in the NFL. During his 20-year career, he played for the San Francisco 49ers, Oakland Raiders, and Seattle Seahawks.

Rice had an incredible ability to catch passes and run precise routes, and set numerous records in the NFL.

It is known that Rice had a ritual of wearing the same pair of football gloves throughout the entire season.

This is because football gloves are an important part of a receiver's equipment and provide enhanced grip on the ball, allowing players to catch passes more easily.

Rice was also known for his work ethic and dedication to training.

He spent hours practicing routes and working on his game during the offseason, which helped him stay at the top of his game for so many years.

In his career, Rice won three Super Bowls, was selected to the Pro Bowl 13 times, and was named first-team All-Pro 11 times.

He also set several NFL records, including the record for most receiving yards in a career and the record for most touchdowns scored in a career.

After retiring, Rice was inducted into the Professional Football Hall of Fame.

93

Drew Brees.

He is a former NFL quarterback who played the majority
of his career with the New Orleans Saints.

Throughout his career, Brees had a great deal of rituals
and habits that helped him prepare for games.

It is known that Brees followed a rigorous and controlled diet
before games, and often ate baked chicken with brown
rice the night before a game.

This is because chicken meat is a rich source of protein, while
brown rice is rich in complex carbohydrates, which help
provide sustained energy during the game.

In addition to his diet, Brees also had a specific warm-up
routine before each game, which included a throwing
session and stretching.

He was also known for being an inspiring leader
on the field and for his tireless work ethic.

Brees won a Super Bowl with the Saints in the 2009-2010
season, was selected to the Pro Bowl 13 times, and set
numerous records in the NFL, including the record
for most career completions.

After retiring from the NFL, Brees has devoted himself to
philanthropy and is a prominent community activist
in the city of New Orleans.

94

Adrian Peterson.

He is a former NFL running back who spent much of his career with the Minnesota Vikings.

It is known that Peterson had a series of rituals and habits that helped him prepare for games.

One of these rituals was that he always wore the same combination of underwear before a game.

Peterson believed that underwear was an important part of his gear and that wearing the same combination every time made him feel comfortable and confident on the field.

In addition to his choice of underwear, Peterson also had a specific warm-up routine before games, which included stretching and a ball-throwing session.

He was also known as a very focused and disciplined player, and he prepared intensely both physically and mentally for games.

Peterson is considered one of the greatest runners in NFL history, having won the NFL Offensive Player of the Year Award twice and being selected to the Pro Bowl eight times.

He has also set numerous records in the NFL, including the record for most rushing yards in a season and the record for most consecutive games with 100 or more rushing yards.

95

Bill Belichick.

He is one of the most successful coaches
in the history of the NFL.

He began his career as an assistant coach with the Baltimore
Colts in 1975 and has been the head coach of the
New England Patriots since 2000.

During his time with the Patriots, he has led the team to six
Super Bowl victories and has been named NFL Coach
of the Year three times.

Belichick is known for his defensive playing style and has
developed several tactical innovations throughout his career.

He is also known for his ability to prepare his team for games,
and for his meticulous focus on analyzing the
opposing team's strategy.

However, Belichick has also been the subject of
controversy throughout his career.

In 2007, the Patriots were penalized for recording the defensive
signals of the New York Jets, which led to a fine
and the loss of a draft pick.

In 2015, the Patriots were accused of using deflated footballs
during a game, which led to another fine and the
suspension of their quarterback, Tom Brady.

Despite these controversies, Belichick remains one of the most
respected coaches in the NFL and continues to lead
the Patriots to success in the league.

96

Vince Lombardi.

He is widely regarded as one of the most successful and respected coaches in the history of the NFL.

He was born in Brooklyn, New York in 1913 and began his coaching career at Fordham University in 1947.

Later, he worked as an assistant coach for the New York Giants and the Green Bay Packers before being named head coach of the Packers in 1959.

During his time with the Packers, Lombardi built a dominant team that won five NFL championships in seven years, including the first two Super Bowls.

His focus on discipline, team mentality, and hard work became a hallmark of his leadership.

In addition to his success on the field, Lombardi is remembered for his inspiring quotes, including "hard work doesn't guarantee success, but without it, there's no chance" and "winners never quit and quitters never win."

Unfortunately, Lombardi passed away at the age of 57 in 1970 due to intestinal cancer, but his legacy as a coach and leader continues to inspire players, coaches, and fans alike.

In his honor, the Super Bowl trophy bears his name.

97

Don Shula.

He is considered one of the most successful
coaches in NFL history.

He was born in 1930 in Ohio and began his career as a player
at John Carroll University before being hired by the
Cleveland Browns in 1951.

Although he didn't play for very long, Shula decided to become
a coach and started as an assistant at
several universities and NFL teams.

In 1963, Shula became the head coach of the Baltimore Colts
and led the team to a record of 12-2 and an appearance
in the NFL championship game that year.

After an unfortunate ending to his career with the Colts, Shula
joined the Miami Dolphins in 1970 and led the team to a
record of 14-0 in the regular season of 1972, the only
perfect season in NFL history.

Shula led the Dolphins to two Super Bowl victories
and five appearances in the same event.

Shula retired after the 1995 season with a head
coaching record of 347 wins, 173 losses, and 6 ties.

He was inducted into the Pro Football Hall of Fame in
1997 and is remembered as one of the greatest
coaches in the history of the sport.

Shula passed away in May 2020 at the age of 90.

98

Chuck Noll.

He is considered one of the most successful coaches in NFL history.

He was the head coach of the Pittsburgh Steelers from 1969 until 1991, becoming the longest-tenured coach in team history.

During his career, Noll led the Steelers to four Super Bowl titles (in the 1974, 1975, 1978, and 1979 seasons), making them one of the most dominant teams of the 1970s.

He was also the first head coach to win four Super Bowls, a record that stood for many years.

In addition to his on-field achievements, Noll is remembered for his philosophy of "building from the inside out," which meant he believed in building a strong team through careful player selection and the formation of a coherent system of play.

He passed away in 2014 at the age of 82.

99

Bill Walsh.

He is one of the most influential coaches
in the history of the NFL.

Born in California in 1931, Walsh became the head coach
of the San Francisco 49ers in 1979.

He was the creator of the West Coast offense, which was
characterized by an intensive use of short and medium
passes, instead of relying on long passing plays.

Under Walsh's leadership, the 49ers won three Super
Bowls in the 1980s, including one in 1982,
one in 1985, and one in 1989.

He also led the team to six division titles and three
appearances in the NFC Championship Game.

In addition to being an innovator on offense, Walsh
was also known for his ability to develop talent.

During his time in San Francisco, he coached future NFL
stars such as Joe Montana, Jerry Rice, and Steve Young.

Walsh retired as head coach in 1989, but continued to work
in football as an analyst and mentor to young coaches.

He passed away in 2007 due to leukemia.

100

Tom Landry.

He was a famous head football coach in the NFL,
best known for his time with the Dallas Cowboys.

Born in Texas in 1924, Landry served in the United States Air
Force during World War II before beginning his career in football.

Landry started as a player in the NFL in 1949, playing for
the New York Yankees and the New York Giants.

After retiring as a player in 1955, Landry began working as
an assistant coach, first with the Giants and then with
the Dallas Texans (later the Kansas City Chiefs).

In 1960, Landry was named head coach of the Dallas Cowboys,
an expansion team in the NFL.

During his 29 years as head coach of the Cowboys, Landry led
the team to 20 winning seasons, 13 playoff appearances,
and two Super Bowl victories.

Landry was known for being an innovator on defense,
especially with his "Flex Defense."

He was also a pioneer in the use of technology to analyze
the game and improve team preparation.

After his retirement in 1989, Landry remained involved
in football as a commentator and advisor.

He passed away in 2000 at the age of 75.

101

Joe Gibbs.

He is a former head football coach who spent much of his career with the NFL's Washington Redskins.

He is widely regarded as one of the most successful coaches in the history of professional football.

Gibbs served as the head coach of the Redskins in two different stints: from 1981 to 1992 and from 2004 to 2007.

During his time with the Redskins, Gibbs led the team to three Super Bowl championships in 1982, 1987, and 1991.

He also achieved four Super Bowl appearances in total.

In addition, Gibbs was the head coach during the Redskins' record of 10-win seasons eight times in a nine-year period.

Gibbs is also known for being an innovator in the offensive game and for his ability to bring out the best in his players.

He is also known for his strong work ethic and his commitment to the Christian faith, which he often incorporated into his approach to the game and the culture of his team.

If you have enjoyed the curiosities of the NFL presented in this book, we would like to ask you to share a review on Amazon.

Your opinion is very valuable to us and to other American football enthusiasts who are looking to be entertained and learn new knowledge about this sport.

We understand that leaving a comment can be a tedious process, but we ask you to take a few minutes of your time to share your thoughts and opinions with us.

Your support is very important to us and it helps us continue creating quality content for fans of this incredible sport.

We appreciate your support and hope that you have enjoyed reading our book as much as we enjoyed writing it.

Thank you for sharing your experience with us!

★ ★ ★ ★ ★